MASTER PROCRASTINATION & ACHIEVE YOUR GOALS

8 Essential Steps to Regain Control of Your Life

MATTHEW LIN

Acknowledgments

Writing a book is a journey involving the contributions, support, and encouragement of numerous individuals who come together to make the final creation possible. As I reflect on the completion of this work, I am filled with gratitude for the many people who have played a role in bringing these pages to life.

First and foremost, I extend heartfelt appreciation to my family: Aun, Christian, and Christa. Your unwavering love, encouragement, and understanding laid the foundation upon which I built this endeavor, with your belief in me and sacrifices made affording me the time and space necessary to dive into this project with full dedication.

To my friends and colleagues, thank you for your enthusiasm, insightful discussions, and constructive feedback. Your perspectives enriched the content of this book and helped shape its final form, while your willingness to lend an ear and offer your expertise has been truly invaluable.

I also am deeply indebted to the professionals who contributed their expertise to this project. Kevin, your insights and guidance with respect to this topic were instrumental in shaping the depth and accuracy of the content. Your commitment to excellence is truly commendable.

My gratitude extends to Rica Graphics @ricacabrex for the outstanding cover design and interior layout. Your creative vision and attention to detail have given this book a visual identity that beautifully complements its content.

I also extend my thanks to Kerri Marikakis for your meticulous editing and careful review of the manuscript. Your expertise and dedication ensured the text is polished, coherent, and engaging.

Lastly, I want to express my heartfelt appreciation to you, my readers. Your interest in this book is both humbling and inspiring, and it is my sincere hope that the insights and techniques shared within these pages will contribute positively to your personal and professional journey.

In closing, I acknowledge everyone who has contributed to this book, both directly and indirectly. Your belief in the importance of personal growth, productivity, and emotional well-being has driven me to share these ideas with the world. May our collective efforts ripple out and create positive change in the lives of those who engage with this work.

With heartfelt thanks,
Matthew Lin
September 2023

Contents

Overcoming procrastination is a common challenge many people face in their daily lives.

Procrastination can hinder productivity, increase stress, and prevent you from reaching your goals. Fortunately, you can implement a series of effective strategies to stop procrastination in its tracks and make the most of your time.

Diving right in, here are eight steps to help you conquer procrastination:

Chapter 1, Step 1: Set Clear Goals

Define your short-term and long-term goals. A clear understanding of what you want to achieve gives you motivation and direction, making it easier to stay focused and avoid distractions.

Chapter 2, Step 2: Break Down Tasks into Smaller Steps

Large tasks often feel overwhelming, leading to procrastination. Break these down into smaller, manageable steps, with this approach making them feel less daunting and helping you maintain a sense of accomplishment as you complete each one.

Chapter 3, Step 3: Prioritize Tasks

Determine which tasks are most important and time-sensitive, employing techniques such as the Eisenhower Matrix to categorize tasks based on urgency and importance. Tackling high-priority tasks first prevents procrastination and ensures critical work is accomplished.

Chapter 4, Step 4: Create a Schedule

Develop a daily or weekly schedule that outlines when you'll work on specific tasks, allocating dedicated time slots for work, breaks, and leisure activities. A structured routine helps minimize procrastination by establishing a consistent work rhythm.

Chapter 5, Step 5: Utilize Time Management Techniques

Employ techniques such as the Pomodoro Technique, which involves working for a set period followed by a short break. This approach can increase focus and productivity by breaking tasks down into manageable intervals.

Chapter 6, Step 6: Eliminate Distractions

Identify common distractions in your environment such as social media, noise, or clutter. Minimize or eliminate these distractions during work periods and consider using website blockers or apps that limit access to time-wasting websites.

Chapter 7, Step 7: Practice Self-Compassion

Be kind to yourself and avoid self-criticism, knowing negative self-talk can contribute to procrastination by creating feelings of guilt and inadequacy. Treat setbacks as learning opportunities and focus on progress rather than perfection.

Chapter 8, Step 8: Reward Yourself

Establish a reward system for completing tasks and achieving milestones. Celebrate your accomplishments—whether by enjoying a treat, taking a break, or engaging in a fun activity— as positive reinforcement can motivate you to stay on track and overcome procrastination.

Remember that overcoming procrastination is a gradual process requiring patience and consistent effort. Experiment with these steps to pinpoint strategies that work best for *you*, adapting these to your unique needs and circumstances. With the right amount of determination and practice, you can develop effective habits to help overcome procrastination and achieve your goals.

Introduction

In the intricate tapestry of human existence, the struggle against procrastination stands out as a perennial challenge: a battle fought within the recesses of our minds and at the boundaries of our ambitions. It is a universal adversary, cunningly disguised as a fleeting moment of leisure or a harmless delay yet wielding the power to erode the very foundations of our dreams. As we grapple with the allure that comes with putting things off, we often find ourselves trapped in a cycle of unrealized potential, untapped creativity, and unfulfilled aspirations.

Master Procrastination & Achieve Your Goals: 8 Essential Steps to Regain Control of Your Life is not just a book; it is a guiding light illuminating a path toward a life free from the clutches of procrastination as you reclaim sovereignty over your actions. This journey is an exploration of the human psyche and one that unveils the intricacies of motivation, self-discipline, and the profound art of achieving your most cherished goals.

On the pages that follow, we'll embark on an odyssey of self-discovery and empowerment—a voyage that transcends traditional time management techniques and delves into the very heart of *why* we procrastinate. We will unravel the psychological forces that drive this tendency and, more importantly, unveil a comprehensive arsenal of strategies to counteract them.

You will also become intimately familiar with eight essential steps that serve as beacons to guide you through the labyrinth of procrastination toward the shores of achievement. From decoding the intricate psychology of procrastination and igniting the flame of intrinsic motivation to sculpting a crystal-clear vision of your aspirations and crafting actionable plans/mastering the art of prioritization, this guide is your compass to navigate the tumultuous waters of self-doubt and hesitation.

Rest assured: you are not alone on this journey. The history of humanity is punctuated by individuals who, despite grappling with the same adversary, have ultimately triumphed: artists who paint masterpieces, inventors who birth innovations, and leaders who carve a path to greatness. Their stories—alongside timeless wisdom and cutting-edge insights—will serve as beacons of inspiration, guiding you toward a life of purpose, achievement, and fulfillment.

As we delve into the nuances of each step, I urge you to approach this voyage with an open heart and eager mind as you prepare to confront the inner narratives that have held you back, embrace discomfort, and forge new habits aligning with your aspirations. On the forthcoming pages, you'll find not only the knowledge to conquer procrastination but also the tools to forge a path toward self-mastery.

With determination as our compass and the eight essential steps as our guideposts, let's embark on this transformative journey together. As we navigate the labyrinth of procrastination, we shall emerge: not as its victims but instead its conquerors, empowered to reclaim control of our lives, manifest our boldest dreams, and unfurl the tapestry of our own success.

Step 1

SET CLEAR GOALS

"Set clear goals and watch as the universe conspires to align itself with your aspirations."

-Oprah Winfrey

Oprah Winfrey has left an indelible impression on people around the globe as a media tycoon, talk show host, actress, and philanthropist given her myriad successful endeavors and motivational speeches. The famous quote above sums up Oprah's outlook on the interconnectivity of all things and the power of intention and resolve.

Born in Kosciusko, Mississippi on January 29, 1954, Oprah endured a difficult upbringing marred by poverty and adversity but went on to become a major figure in the entertainment world. Her career in fact began in high school—when she worked at a local radio station—and culminated with her breakthrough on *The*

Oprah Winfrey Show. For its entire 25-year run, the show served as a forum for thoughtful debate on questions delving into identity, community, and individual development. In combination with her authentic compassion and sensitivity, Oprah's extraordinary talent for connecting with her audience has won the hearts of so many people around the world.

Her belief that one's thoughts, actions, and outcomes are all interconnected is reflected in her comment regarding the importance of goal-setting. The law of attraction—a philosophy proposing that one's ideas ultimately create his or her own reality—provides the foundation for this viewpoint. The importance of this personal clarity and intention in constructing one's path is central to Oprah's perspective, which extends beyond the mystical parts of this ethos.

Clearly articulating one's wants and needs is an essential step in the goal-setting process, and individuals who initiate this endeavor give themselves a guide for how to move forward. With this type of insight, individuals can successfully maintain concentration, make well-informed choices, and steer their efforts towards their goals. Oprah's life is a testament to the effectiveness of goal-setting; she worked tirelessly to make her childhood dream of becoming a famous talk show host a reality.

By focusing on our goals and working hard in pursuit of them, we can help align invisible forces in our favor—as suggested by the belief that the universe conspires to align itself with ambitions. With this in mind, there's a need to not merely hope things will work out but instead engage in active participation and thoughtful decision-making with an optimistic outlook. Oprah's life truly speaks to the power of positive thinking and determined action.

In addition to rising to fame in the entertainment world, Oprah has served as a leader in the realms of philanthropy, social justice, and education while also maintaining her dedication to helping disadvantaged youth by opening the Oprah Winfrey Leadership Academy for Girls in South Africa. Her charitable work exemplifies the idea that when people set their minds to do some good in this world, the universe conspires to make that happen.

Ultimately, Oprah Winfrey's quote reflects her outlook on the interconnectivity of intentions, behaviors, and results while her life and accomplishments help demonstrate what one can accomplish with determination and dedication. By visualizing an ideal future and working tirelessly towards that end, one can unlock the universe's latent dynamics and pave the way for his or her heart's desire.

Just as a ship needs a precise destination to navigate the open sea, individuals require well-defined goals to steer their life's journey. By establishing clear goals, we arm ourselves with a roadmap, sense of purpose, and target for our efforts. The universe conspiring, meanwhile, implies that opportunities and circumstances tend to fall into place when our intentions are crystal clear: propelling us toward our desired outcomes. Oprah's wisdom reminds us that by setting clear goals, we play an active role in shaping our destiny and inviting the forces of success to work in our favor.

In the grand tapestry of human aspirations, the art of setting clear goals serves as the weaver's loom whereby the threads of intention, determination, and accomplishment meticulously intertwine. Just as a navigator charts a course across uncharted waters, setting clear goals acts as a compass that directs our efforts, shapes our actions, and guides us toward the destinations we yearn to reach.

Imagine embarking on a journey without a map or destination in mind. While the path may perhaps intrigue us, the lack of direction can cause us to wander aimlessly—unsure of where we're headed or how to gauge our progress. Setting clear goals is akin to casting a guiding light on our path, illuminating the way and instilling a sense of purpose that propels us forward despite any challenges or setbacks.

Whether we seek personal growth, professional advancement, or the fulfillment of lifelong dreams, defining clear goals empowers us to translate our aspirations into tangible, achievable objectives: transforming vague wishes into focused targets, mere dreams into actionable plans, and sparks into sustained flames of motivation.

In this chapter, we'll delve into the art and science of setting clear goals: unraveling the intricacies of articulating aspirations with precision and identifying the steps necessary to turn a vision into reality. From the psychology behind effective goal-setting to the strategies that ensure goals remain attainable, we will explore every facet of this essential skill.

Prepare to embark on a journey of intention, foresight, and empowerment. In setting clear goals, you'll uncover tools and insights that will empower you to sculpt a future aligning with your deepest desires. With each and every word, let's illuminate the path toward achieving clarity, direction, and ultimate success.

Overall, setting clear goals is a fundamental step towards triumph and maintaining focus in various aspects of life: providing motivation and a sense of purpose while helping you make informed decisions and prioritize your efforts with precision. Whether with respect to personal development, career advancement, or any other endeavor, this process is a powerful tool for success.

Here's why setting clear goals is important (and how to do so effectively!):

Importance of Setting Clear Goals:

1. Focus and Direction: Clear goals act as a roadmap for your actions and heighten your sense of direction, helping you channel your energy and efforts toward achieving specific outcomes.

2. Motivation: Goals serve as powerful motivators, providing a clear vision of what you want to achieve and thus increasing the likelihood you'll stay committed and overcome challenges along the way.

3. Measurable Progress: Clear goals are often measurable and allow you to track your progress and see how far you've come, giving you a sense of achievement that can boost your confidence and keep you motivated.

4. Effective Decision-Making: Well-defined goals make decisions easier, feeding your ability to assess whether a choice aligns with your goals and contributes to your overall vision.

5. Time Management: You can prioritize tasks and allocate your time more efficiently with clear goals, focusing on activities that directly contribute to your objectives while avoiding time-wasting distractions.

6. Accountability: Clearly articulated goals make it easier for others to understand your intentions and provide support or feedback, with this accountability encouraging you to stay on track.

Tips for Setting Clear Goals:

1. Be Specific: Clearly define your goals in precise terms. Avoid vague statements and focus on what you want to achieve, how you will do it, and the desired outcome.

2. Make Goals Measurable: Quantifiable goals allow you to track progress and success. Include specific criteria that indicate when you've achieved your objective.

3. Set Achievable Goals: While aiming high is important, make sure your ambitions are realistic and attainable. Setting overly ambitious goals can lead to frustration and discouragement.

4. Remember Relevance: Your goals should be applicable to your overall aspirations. Ensure they align with your values, long-term objectives, and desired direction for your personal and/or work life.

5. Establish Time-Bound Goals: Set a clear timeframe for achieving your aims. Deadlines create a sense of urgency and help you stay focused on making consistent progress.

6. Break Down Larger Goals: If a goal feels overwhelming, break it down into smaller, manageable steps. This approach makes your objective more achievable and allows you to celebrate milestones along the way.

7. Put Pen to Paper: Writing down your goals solidifies your commitment and serves as a constant reminder of what you're working towards.

8. Visualize Success: Imagine yourself achieving your goals. Visualization can boost motivation and enhance your belief in your ability to succeed.

9. Review and Adjust: Regularly review your goals and assess your progress. Make adjustments as necessary based on evolving circumstances or new insights gained.

Setting clear goals is a skill that takes practice and refinement. By incorporating these principles into your daily life, you can harness the power of goal-setting to drive your success and achieve the outcomes you desire.

Step 2

BREAK TASKS DOWN INTO SMALLER STEPS

"Divide and conquer: Break tasks into smaller steps, for in their accomplishment lies the true mastery of achievement."

-Leonardo da Vinci

Leonardo da Vinci, a true Renaissance polymath of the Middle Ages, is hailed as one of the greatest minds in history and left an unmistakable imprint on several fields with his artistic talent, scientific curiosity, and inventiveness. As exemplified by his wise quote shared above, he employed a practical approach when seeking to overcome obstacles and possessed an awareness of the road to mastery.

Leonardo da Vinci demonstrated a hunger for knowledge from an early age, with this boundless appetite prompting him to dabble in several disciplines including art, anatomy, engineering, mathematics, and more. His journals attest to his insatiable curiosity about the world while his paintings—such as *The Mona Lisa* and *The Last Supper*—are celebrated for their originality and meticulousness.

The quote attributed to Leonardo emphasizes the importance of breaking up difficult jobs into simpler ones. This strategy, often referred to as "divide and conquer," is predicated on the premise that it is much easier to achieve a major goal if that goal is broken down into smaller, more manageable chunks: meaning individuals will feel less overwhelmed and make more consistent progress towards their final goal if they split a complex task into smaller components.

This notion was reflected in Leonardo's own work. When creating his works of art, he gave careful consideration to every last detail, no matter how minute: allowing him to create stunningly realistic and lifelike artwork via a deep awareness of the subtleties of shape, texture, and light. His dedication to learning about human anatomy by breaking it down into more manageable pieces, for example, is reflected in his anatomical research.

Leonardo's inclination to break down complex issues in this manner also had a significant impact on his scientific research and innovations, with his ability to do so for seemingly incomprehensible natural phenomena driving many of his seminal scientific investigations—including those related to flying and hydraulics. This strategy ultimately fed his ability to make important contributions in fields completely unrelated to painting.

"In their accomplishment lies the true mastery of achievement" reflects Leonardo's conviction that genuine mastery is based on a steady accumulation of small victories. Gaining a firm grasp on the fundamentals is therefore the first step towards a thorough and profound understanding of one's field, and in his continuous quest for knowledge and creativity, Leonardo exemplified this principle.

These words still ring true in many spheres of modern life, both private and professional. Whether you're trying to manage a project or foster a talent, the advice to "break it down into smaller steps" provides a systematic and powerful way to navigate complicated and rapidly evolving environments in pursuit of lofty objectives.

Leonardo da Vinci's quote—which sums up his approach to life as well as his practical wisdom—infers individuals can master complex tasks, overcome challenging obstacles, and reach their full potential by breaking the work down into manageable chunks and toiling methodically to execute each one. Leonardo's own diverse creativity is proof positive that this method works, serving as a reminder that great accomplishments are frequently the result of careful, incremental improvement.

In the grand symphony of productivity and accomplishment, there exists a subtle yet powerful melody—an art form that holds the key to converting monumental undertakings into manageable achievements. This art is the skill of breaking tasks into smaller steps, a technique that transforms overwhelming challenges into a harmonious progression of actions and outcomes.

Imagine standing before a towering mountain, its lofty summit shrouded in clouds. The journey to its peak might seem daunting or perhaps even impossible. Yet, with each step taken, the mountain becomes conquerable. Breaking tasks into smaller steps is akin to embarking on a series of purposeful hikes up that very same mountain, allowing us to ascend with confidence and celebrate each milestone along the way.

In this chapter, we'll embark on a journey of deconstruction and reconstruction that empowers us to dismantle complex undertakings into manageable components and reconstruct them into a symphony of achievement. We'll also delve into the psychology behind this technique, exploring how it helps inertia evolve into action and uncertainty into clarity.

From the intricacies of planning to the psychology of progress, we'll unravel the threads that weave together this transformative strategy. Whether you're facing a colossal project, pursuing a personal goal, or striving for professional success, the ability to break tasks into smaller steps is a cornerstone of productivity and an essential tool in your toolbox.

Prepare to dive into the art of deconstruction and reconstruction—turning daunting challenges into step-by-step triumphs in the process—and let the pages ahead serve as your guide to unlocking the potential within each task, illuminating the path forward and revealing the beauty of progress that emerges as you break free from the confines of complexity.

Let's embark on this journey of transformation, *together*. As we break tasks into smaller steps, this action becomes the catalyst for monumental achievements and a symphony of progress.

It's also a powerful strategy to increase productivity, stifle overwhelm, and conquer procrastination. In transforming daunting projects into manageable and achievable actions, this approach makes it easier to stay focused and motivated. Whether you're tackling a work assignment, personal project, or even a household chore, you'll be delighted to see consistent progress while employing this strategy.

Here's why it's so effective (and how to implement it!):

Benefits of Breaking Tasks into Smaller Steps:

1. Reduces Overwhelm: As large tasks are often intimidating, breaking them down into smaller steps makes them feel more attainable—reducing stress and anxiety.

2. Enhances Focus: Smaller tasks are easier to focus on, allowing you to concentrate your attention and energy more effectively and often leading to improved concentration and work quality.

3. Boosts Motivation: Accomplishing smaller steps provides a sense of fulfillment and the drive to continue working, with each completed step serving as a mini milestone that encourages you to keep going.

4. Establishes a Clear Action Plan: Breaking tasks down creates a clear roadmap for how to proceed, eliminating ambiguity and uncertainty and clarifying next steps.

5. Encourages Consistency: It's more manageable to fit smaller steps into your daily routine, with their consistent completion leading to steady progress over time.

Implementing this Strategy:

1. Identify the Task: Begin by clearly defining the larger task or project you want to complete. This could take shape as writing a report, organizing your closet, or learning a new skill.

2. List Subtasks: Break your primary task into smaller, actionable subtasks. Each one should be a concrete action that moves you closer to achieving your larger goal.

3. Prioritize and Order: Arrange your subtasks in a logical sequence. Consider what needs to be done first, what follows, and so on, forming a step-by-step plan of action.

4. Set Timeframes: Assign an estimated timetable to each subtask. This will help you effectively allocate your time and prevent you from spending too much time on any single step.

5. Start Small: Begin with the first subtask and focus solely on its completion. Starting with a small, manageable step can help build momentum and overcome initial resistance.

6. Celebrate Progress: As you complete each subtask, take a moment to acknowledge your achievement. This positive reinforcement can boost your motivation to proceed to the next step.

7. Review and Adjust: Regularly review your progress and adjust your plan if needed. As you work through each step, you may gain insights that warrant modifications.

8. Stay Flexible: While it's important to follow your plan, remain open to adjustments based on unforeseen challenges or new information that presents itself.

Breaking tasks into smaller steps is a practical and effective approach to managing your workload and achieving your goals. By adopting this strategy, you can build a sense of accomplishment, maintain focus, and consistently make progress toward your objectives: ultimately leading to improved productivity and success.

Step 3

PRIORITIZE TASKS

"Productivity is the art of prioritizing tasks; like a sculptor chiseling away the unnecessary, we carve a masterpiece of achievement."

-Stephen Covey

Author, professor, and motivational speaker Stephen Covey is perhaps best known for writing *The 7 Habits of Highly Effective People*. His lessons have had a significant effect on both individual and organizational growth, emphasizing concepts that enable people to live more meaningful and fruitful lives. The quote above from Covey encapsulates his views on productivity, focus, and the transformational power of conscious decision-making.

Born on October 24, 1932, Covey spent his life researching and sharing practices designed to help people become more productive in their personal and professional interactions. His writings, specifically, offer time-tested advice on how to achieve personal happiness and success, and *The 7 Habits of Highly Effective People* (coauthored with James Clear) became an instant classic following its initial publication in 1989.

Covey's quote makes a striking comparison between productivity and sculpture, suggesting we can boost productivity in the same way we can chisel away a block of stone to reveal a masterpiece by carefully selecting and prioritizing jobs. A crucial part of this procedure is differentiating truly necessary tasks from their less important counterparts.

The sculptor analogy underscores the need for deliberate action and precise execution when the goal is increased production. Just as a sculptor's every chisel blow impacts the final product, every decision and action a person makes affects his/her level of success and productivity. Productivity, as this principle illustrates, is not about speed but rather quality and focus on the proper tasks.

The transformational effect of deliberate decision-making means individuals who set priorities and have a clear vision of their goals can carve out a route to success, just as a sculptor perceives the final form before beginning his/her work. To achieve this goal, one must successfully identify activities that are useful vs those that are distracting.

Aligning one's behaviors with one's fundamental principles and ultimate goals is a core tenet of Covey's teachings, with his method centering on developing good habits and stressing practices such as proactivity, thinking about the ultimate result, and prioritizing what's most important. Individuals can therefore utilize these concepts as a map to make choices in support of their goals and development.

Covey's words are as timely now as they were when he first spoke them, as the ability to pinpoint priorities in the face of competing demands is becoming increasingly important. With this in mind, individuals can "chisel away" the unimportant to make room for more pressing endeavors, sharper concentration, and greater productivity.

Stephen Covey's perspective on productivity as a deliberate and purposeful process is wonderfully captured by the afore-mentioned quote, inspiring individuals to mold their productivity—just as a sculptor crafts a masterpiece—by setting priorities and removing any fluff. This wisdom continues to serve as a beacon for those seeking direction in life while helping these folks prioritize what matters most as they forge forward in pursuit of their goals.

In the intricate dance of daily life, a symphony of tasks and responsibilities unfolds before us—each one vying for our attention and energy. The ability to discern between the urgent and the important, the trivial and the crucial, is akin to wielding a conductor's baton, orchestrating the rhythm of our days with precision and purpose. This art is known as task prioritization, a skill that empowers us to allocate our resources effectively while ensuring our efforts align with our goals and aspirations.

Imagine a painter standing before a blank canvas, a palette of vibrant colors at his fingertips. The act of prioritizing tasks is much like selecting the hues and brushstrokes that will shape the masterpiece that ultimately emerges. It's about making deliberate choices that infuse each stroke with intention, culminating in a work of art that reflects clarity, focus, and purpose.

In this chapter, we'll embark on a journey of discernment and decision-making that will equip us with the tools necessary to sift through the myriad tasks vying for our attention: identifying those primed to propel us toward our desired outcomes. From the principles that guide effective prioritization to the strategies ensuring we allocate our time and energy wisely, we will explore every facet of this essential skill.

Whether you're a professional navigating a demanding career, a student juggling academic responsibilities, or an individual yearning to lead a more purposeful life, the art of task prioritization is a cornerstone of productivity and success.

Prepare to delve into the heart of effective decision-making, whereby the act of task prioritization acts as a compass guiding us toward a life imbued with focus, accomplishment, and fulfillment. Each concept we explore will cultivate our ability to discern the crucial from the inconsequential and direct our efforts toward what truly matters.

Together, let's embark on this journey of empowerment whereby the symphony of task prioritization becomes the melody guiding us through the ever-evolving landscape of our lives.

Prioritizing tasks is a crucial skill that empowers you to make the most of your time, accomplish your goals, and manage your responsibilities effectively. With so many demands on your time and attention, it's essential to determine which tasks are most important and urgent overall. This prioritization process will ultimately feed your ability to focus on what truly matters and best allocate your resources.

Here's why prioritization is important (and how to go about it!):

Importance of Task Prioritization:

1. Maximizes Productivity: Prioritizing helps identify tasks that have the greatest impact on your goals and outcomes, allowing you to concentrate your efforts on high-priority tasks and thus maximize your productivity while achieving more meaningful results.

2. Manages Overwhelm: Though it's easy to feel overwhelmed while staring down a lengthy to-do list, prioritization allows you to break down tasks into manageable chunks: reducing stress and making tasks feel more achievable.

3. Enhances Decision-Making: By knowing what needs to be done first, you can make better decisions about how to invest your time and energy: preventing indecision and the feeling of being pulled in multiple directions.

4. Reduces Procrastination: Prioritization helps you tackle important tasks promptly, reducing the likelihood of procrastination and making it more likely you'll start and stay on track given a clear order of to-dos.

5. Improves Time Management: Effective prioritization ensures your time is spent on tasks aligning with your goals, meaning you won't waste time on less important activities.

Prioritization Process:

1. List Tasks: Begin by listing all the tasks you need to complete. This could include work-related projects, personal commitments, and daily chores.

2. Determine Importance: Assess the significance of each task. Consider how each one contributes to your goals, deadlines, and overall well-being.

3. Consider Urgency: Identify tasks that are time-sensitive or have impending deadlines. Assign these a higher priority if they also align with importance.

4. Use the Eisenhower Matrix, dividing tasks into four categories:

    a. Urgent and Important: Perform these tasks immediately.
    b. Important but Not Urgent: Schedule these tasks for later.
    c. Urgent but Not Important: Delegate or minimize time spent on these tasks.
    d. Not Urgent and Not Important: Consider eliminating or postponing these tasks.

5. Evaluate Resources: Consider the resources (time, skills, assistance) required for each task. This can help you decide which ones to tackle first and whether you should delegate or seek help.

6. Rank and Order: Rank tasks based on their importance, urgency, and resource requirements. Establish a clear order in which you'll address them.

7. Create a Schedule: Allocate time blocks in your schedule for each task, based on your prioritized list. Be realistic about the time required for each one.

8. Adapt as Needed: Reassess your priorities as circumstances evolve. New information or shifting deadlines may require adjustments to your task list.

9. Focus on Completion: As you work through your tasks, focus on completing each one individually before moving on to the next step. Multitasking can hinder productivity and dilute your efforts.

10. Reflect and Learn: After completing your tasks, reflect on the outcomes and your overall process. Learn from your experiences to refine your prioritization skills.

Prioritizing tasks is a skill that improves with practice. By consistently evaluating and organizing your tasks, you can make informed decisions, reduce stress, and boost your goal-achieving efficiency.

Step 4

CREATE A SCHEDULE

"Crafting a schedule is not just an arrangement of hours, but a masterpiece of productivity, painted with purpose and framed by discipline."

-Maya Angelou

A renowned poet, memoirist, and civil rights activist, Maya Angelou is admired for her insightful understanding of the human condition and extraordinary gift of putting feelings into words. Her writings have had a lasting impact on readers all over the globe, and the quote above exemplifies her insight regarding the need for discipline, intentionality, and time management in pursuit of one's goals.

After entering this world on April 4, 1928 in St. Louis, Missouri, Angelou went on to overcome several obstacles throughout her lifetime. Her works—such as an autobiographical trilogy beginning with *I Know Why the Caged Bird Sings*—include a frank discussion of her own life and broader topics involving identity, racism, and resiliency. She has truly made an unforgettable impact on literature and society with her profound reflection and poetic eloquence.

Angelou's quote is a wonderful illustration of the notion that scheduling is more than just a matter of allocating time and instead an act of deliberate intention. The comparison to a masterpiece highlights the importance of forethought, originality, and care when developing a schedule, meaning a person's calendar can be built in a way that supports his/her aims and desires—much like how one can paint a picture with carefully selected colors, textures, and brushstrokes.

Angelou's understanding of the value of time and the need to maximize the same is reflected in her decision to use the word "productivity," a term that refers to more than just getting things done but also making positive contributions to one's own development, happiness, and success. By framing one's calendar as a "masterpiece of productivity," Angelou urges people to embrace time management as a tool for enriching their lives and realizing their goals.

"Painted with purpose and framed by discipline," meanwhile, sums up the two essential components of efficient time management: aim and dedication. Every minute counts to an even greater degree when it has meaning and is spent working towards a greater goal, while discipline offers the framework and consistency necessary to stick to a plan and make real headway.

Together, determination and self-control lay the groundwork for a prosperous and satisfying existence. Angelou's words serve as a reminder that while creativity and flexibility have their place, the structure of discipline ultimately transforms a schedule into a tool of achievement.

This quote also serves as a gentle reminder to take a mindful approach to time management in a society wherein bustle and distraction are the norm. When we take charge of our schedules, we make room for pursuits that feed our spirits, move us closer to our goals, and nurture our health and happiness. To do this, we must remain open to making decisions and determined to stick to them despite the presence of competing demands.

The words of Maya Angelou continue to motivate people to view their schedules as more than just a list of tasks to complete; rather, they are a blank slate upon which to build the lives of their dreams. Every day is thus a new opportunity to paint a meaningful and fruitful life, with purpose as the canvas and discipline as the paintbrush.

Not only does this beautiful depiction point to Angelou's thoughts on discipline, purpose, and the value of time management, but it also emphasizes the significance of consciously designing our days and aligning our actions to our goals by comparing this process to the creation of a masterpiece; anyone seeking to make the most of their time on Earth and build a life full of significance and achievement can use this knowledge as a beacon.

Overall, Maya Angelou's quote encapsulates the notion that creating a schedule is an act of deliberate design wherein every activity choice and time slot contributes to the larger canvas of one's life.

In the rhythm of our modern lives, time is our most precious currency. Like a master composer crafting a symphony, the skill of creating a schedule empowers us to harmonize various elements of our day into a seamless orchestration of tasks, responsibilities, and personal pursuits; it is a skill that helps us navigate the complexities of life with grace, ensuring every moment is invested purposefully and meaningfully.

Just as an architect meticulously designs the blueprint of a magnificent structure, creating a schedule helps lay the foundation and construct the framework for our daily lives. It's about striking a balance between our professional commitments, personal aspirations, and moments of rest: ensuring each component fits seamlessly to create a life that is both productive and fulfilling.

In this chapter, we'll embark on a journey of time management and organization—one that equips us with the tools necessary to design a schedule aligning with our goals, values, and priorities. From understanding the psychology of time to mastering the art of effective planning, we will explore the principles and strategies that underpin this essential skill.

Whether you're striving to excel in your career, seeking balance in your personal life, or aiming to make the most of each day, the ability to create a schedule is a cornerstone of productivity and a pathway to success.

Prepare to dive into the art of time allocation and resource optimization. As we navigate the intricacies involved with creating a schedule, you'll discover the power of structure and routine to elevate your productivity, amplify your accomplishments, and infuse your days with a sense of purpose and fulfillment.

Together, let's embark on this journey of empowerment whereby the act of creating a schedule becomes the compass guiding us toward a life that is both purpose-driven and harmoniously balanced.

Creating a schedule is an essential tool for effective time management and productivity, with a well-structured routine helping you allocate time to various tasks, responsibilities, and activities: ensuring you make the most of your day. Whether you're juggling work or personal commitments and/or pursuing personal growth, a schedule is the roadmap for your day that will help you stay organized.

Here's why creating a schedule is important (and how to do it effectively!):

Importance of Schedule Creation:

1. Optimal Time Management: A schedule allows you to allocate time for specific tasks and activities, preventing wasted time and ensuring you focus on what matters most.

2. Reduced Stress: Knowing what to expect and establishing a plan can prevent you from feeling overwhelmed and stressed, providing a sense of control over your day.

3. Prioritization: A well-organized schedule helps you prioritize tasks based on their importance and urgency, allowing you to allocate more time to high-priority activities and resources accordingly.

4. Increased Productivity: A schedule encourages you to stay focused and on track, minimizing distractions and helping you manage your energy levels throughout the day.

5. Work-Life Balance: By allocating time for work, personal activities, and relaxation, a schedule helps you strike a healthy balance between your professional and personal lives.

Creating an Effective Schedule:

1. Set Clear Goals: Start by identifying your goals and priorities. Knowing what you want to achieve will help you structure your schedule around meaningful activities.

2. List Tasks and Activities: Make a list of all tasks you need to accomplish. This includes any work-related responsibilities, personal errands, exercise, social activities, and more.

3. Determine Time Blocks: Estimate the amount of time necessary to complete each task or activity. Be realistic about time requirements and consider factors such as preparation and transition times.

4. Use Time Blocks: Assign specific tasks or activities to each afore-mentioned time block. Use a mix of shorter and longer blocks to accommodate different tasks.

5. Prioritize: Allocate more time to high-priority tasks while ensuring your schedule reflects your goals and values.

6. Include Breaks: Don't forget to schedule short breaks between tasks to rest and recharge. Breaks can also help you maintain focus and prevent burnout.

7. Be Flexible: While having a schedule is important, be prepared to adapt if unexpected events or opportunities arise in the process.

8. Utilize Tools: Digital or physical tools such as calendars, planners, or scheduling apps can help keep track of your schedule.

9. Batch Similar Tasks: Group comparable tasks together into a single time block. This reduces context switching and enhances efficiency.

10. Build in Extra Time: Allow for some buffer time between tasks to account for unforeseen delays or for you to wrap up ongoing activities.

11. Review and Reflect: Regularly review your schedule to ensure you're staying on track and progressing toward your goals. Reflect on what's working well and make adjustments as needed.

12. Set Realistic Expectations: Avoid overloading your schedule with too many tasks. Be realistic about what you can accomplish in a day's time.

Remember that while creating a schedule is important, it's *also* important to strike a balance between structure and flexibility; a well-designed schedule should help you achieve your goals while still allowing room for spontaneity and enjoyment. As you practice creating and following schedules, you'll more successfully manage your time and achieve your desired outcomes.

Step 5

UTILIZE TIME MANAGEMENT TECHNIQUES

"Time is the currency of life, and wise is the one who invests it with the precision of time management techniques. Just as a skilled conductor orchestrates a symphony, so must we harmonize our tasks and aspirations to create a masterpiece of productivity and fulfillment."

-Benjamin Franklin

As a Founding Father of the United States, Benjamin Franklin is remembered for his myriad accomplishments across many fields: with his words and guidance influencing generations given his wisdom and insight. As one such example, his philosophy on time, the significance of time management, and the art of creating a balanced and meaningful existence is encapsulated in the quote above.

Though most people associate Franklin with his work involving electricity, he also helped design the United States Constitution and advance several other useful technologies. He was also known as a polymath and a practical philosopher due to his inquisitive nature, diligent work ethic, and ability to think strategically.

By comparing time to money, Franklin highlights both its scarcity and value as something one must manage intelligently and prudently: with the end goal of boosting one's own sense of progress, accomplishment, and fulfillment.

Franklin's emphasis on the "precision of time management techniques" is indicative of his no-nonsense approach to planning. He was in fact well-known for his emphasis on organization, goal-setting, and planning, and his "to-do list" (as a historical artifact) exemplifies his commitment to time management efficiency. Frankin's insights on the nature of productivity and time management also support current strategies used to get more done in less time.

Managing one's time, energy, and focus is both sophisticated and artistic—much like the work of a symphony conductor—and involves bringing together one's obligations, ambitions, and hobbies in pursuit of a balanced and meaningful life in the same way a conductor unifies a diverse group of musicians to create a harmonious and cohesive performance. The term "orchestration" refers to a method of planning and executing activities so they work together in harmony.

The idea of crafting a "masterpiece of productivity and fulfillment," meanwhile, is indicative of Franklin's comprehensive view of success. As he realized that the ability to thrive in one area of life doesn't guarantee happiness in another (and that a full life requires attention to *all* aspects of one's self), this goal is consistent with Franklin's conviction that developing one's character and bettering oneself are necessary for fulfillment.

Franklin's words continue to serve as a guiding light in today's environment—one in which time is often splintered by distractions and competing demands—as well as a timely reminder of the need for mindful time management, the relevance of linking daily tasks to broader goals, and the skill of balancing competing demands.

Benjamin Franklin's quote truly says it all with respect to time management, productivity, and finding one's true calling: analogizing time to money and the balance/coordination of one's life to a conductor directing a symphony. His wisdom continues to motivate people to live their lives with purpose, making the most of the valuable resource that is their time.

In the fast-paced tapestry of modern life, time is the canvas upon which we paint our aspirations, achievements, and moments of joy. Just as an artist wields a brush to create a masterpiece, the skill of time management allows us to paint our days with precision and purpose. It is a skill that transcends the boundaries of mere clock-watching, guiding us to make the most of every precious moment and transform our hours into a beautiful mosaic of accomplishments.

Consider a seasoned conductor leading a symphony orchestra, each movement and note carefully orchestrated to create a harmonious composition. Employing time management techniques is akin to wielding that same conductor's baton, skillfully orchestrating the elements of our day to create a melody of productivity, creativity, and fulfillment.

In this chapter, we'll embark on a journey of mastery—one that equips us with effective techniques and strategies to make time work *for* us rather than *against* us. From the principles underlying effective time management to practical tools that enhance efficiency and focus, we'll delve into the art and science of optimizing how we use our time.

Whether you're a professional looking to advance your career, a student striving to balance academic and personal pursuits, or an individual yearning for a more purposeful life, the ability to harness time is a fundamental key to success.

Prepare to immerse yourself in the realm of time mastery. As we explore the intricacies of time management techniques, you'll uncover the power of intention, the art of prioritization, and the skill of maintaining focus in the face of any distractions. Each technique will ultimately serve as a brushstroke that adds depth and brilliance to the canvas of your life.

Together, let's embark on this journey of empowerment wherein the act of utilizing time management techniques melds into a symphony of purpose, productivity, and possibility.

At their core, time management techniques are valuable strategies that help you make the most of your available time while boosting your productivity and achieving your goals efficiently. They add structure, focus, and discipline to your daily routine, enabling you to work *smarter* rather than *harder*. By incorporating effective time management techniques, you can reduce stress, avoid procrastination, and maintain a healthy work-life balance.

Here are some benefits of popular time management techniques (and how to implement them!):

1. Enhanced Productivity: Time management techniques streamline your activities, enabling you to focus on high-priority tasks and thus ensuring you allocate your energy and effort to endeavors that generate meaningful outcomes—leading to heightened productivity.

2. Reduced Stress: A well-organized schedule minimizes the chaos and overwhelm often associated with an overloaded to-do list as you can allocate time for each task, reducing stress and approaching challenges with a clear, composed mindset.

3. Goal Achievement: Time management techniques— which transform vague aspirations into concrete achievements—allow you to set specific goals and break them down into actionable steps, creating a roadmap for success and giving you a sense of accomplishment when you achieve these milestones.

4. Effective Decision-Making: In managing your time efficiently, you create opportunities for deliberate decision-making and are encouraged to consider your priorities, weigh all options, and make informed choices in alignment with your goals.

5. Improved Work-Life Balance: Incorporating time management techniques enables you to allocate time not only to work but also personal interests, relationships,

and self-care—with this balanced approach nurturing your overall well-being and preventing burnout.

How to Implement Time Management Techniques:

1. Set Clear Goals: Define both short-term and long-term goals, ensuring they're specific, measurable, achievable, relevant, and time-bound (SMART). Your goals will lay the foundation to manage your time effectively.

2. Prioritize Tasks: List all your tasks and categorize them based on their importance and urgency. The afore-mentioned Eisenhower Matrix (based on this principle) can help you prioritize tasks and make decisions about how to allocate your time.

3. Create a Schedule: Enlist the help of digital tools, planners, or calendars to map out your schedule, allocating specific time blocks for tasks, meetings, and personal activities. Be sure to include breaks to reset and recharge.

4. Utilize Time-Blocking: Assign dedicated time slots for specific tasks or groups of tasks. This will prevent you from overloading your schedule while also allowing you to focus on one task at a time.

5. Limit Distractions: Identify potential disruptions and take measures to minimize them. Turn off notifications,

designate specific times to check email or social media, and create an environment that fosters focused work.

6. Practice Single-Tasking: Devote your complete attention to one task at a time, knowing that multitasking can reduce work efficiency and quality. Single-tasking, on the other hand, improves concentration and effectiveness.

7. Reflect and Adjust: Regularly review your schedule and assess your progress. Reflect on what worked well and where improvements are needed, adjusting your time management approach based on these observations.

8. Delegate and Outsource: Recognize tasks ripe for delegation or outsourcing to others. This decision frees up your time for higher-priority activities while leveraging the collective strengths of your team.

9. Learn to Say "No": Be mindful of your commitments and avoid overloading yourself. Politely decline tasks or requests that don't align with your goals or current priorities.

10. Practice Self-Care: Allocate time for relaxation, exercise, hobbies, and quality time with loved ones. Nurturing your physical and mental well-being enhances your overall productivity.

11. Seek Continuous Improvement: Stay open to the idea of adopting new techniques and/or refining existing

ones. Embrace a growth mindset and continuously seek ways to optimize your time management skills.

Experiment with these time management techniques to isolate the strategies that best suit your preferences and work style, mixing and matching as appropriate. Combining multiple techniques can also enhance their effectiveness, with their consistent application ultimately helping you manage your time, boost your productivity, and achieve your goals more efficiently.

Step 6

ELIMINATE DISTRACTIONS

"Conquer the cacophony of distractions, and you shall unveil the masterpiece hidden within your focus."

-Albert Einstein

Brilliant physicist and one of history's most consequential scientists, Albert Einstein is revered for his game-changing contributions to our knowledge of the cosmos. Einstein's knowledge and ideas extended beyond his scientific achievements to other areas of life, however, including productivity and attention. The wisdom reflected in the quote above demonstrates his appreciation for the role that focus, clarity, and the absence of distractions play as we look to achieve significant goals.

Innovating in the realms of physics and mathematics, Albert Einstein changed the world on March 14, 1879 when he was born in Ulm, Germany. Awarded the Nobel Prize in Physics in

1921, he went on to become synonymous with creative brilliance and successfully solve many puzzles of the cosmos and the mind thanks to his out-of-the-box thinking.

In telling his audience to "conquer the cacophony of distractions," Einstein and his words have more relevance now than ever before in an era dominated by nonstop information flows and technological diversions—with "cacophony" used to describe the incessant, discordant sounds of modern life that can cause us to lose focus on what's important. Einstein truly recognizes the need to regain command of one's attention and concentration amidst these circumstances.

One interpretation of the phrase "unveil the masterpiece hidden within your focus" is that intense concentration can spark extraordinary results. Einstein understood the need for focused thought to summon novel solutions in difficult situations, and just as an artist reveals a masterpiece through slow, methodical brushstrokes, so too may an individual reveal his or her own potential and brilliance via sustained, undistracted effort.

The concept of "flow," whereby people are so engrossed in what they're doing that time seems to stand still, is consistent with Einstein's discovery. When you're in the zone, you're more likely to be creative, get more done, and feel good about yourself. Individuals who enter this state of flow can maximize their potential by eliminating distractions.

Beyond his professional career, Einstein's outlook on concentration and diversion is profound. He in fact attributed much of his success to his capacity for intense focus, and his commitment to learning and dedicating time to introspective reflection were crucial to his progress.

In this age of constant distractions, Einstein's words are a helpful reminder to train oneself to engage in willful concentration as we recognize that the greatest works of art are created in the quiet of focused endeavor—far from the distractions that can derail our efforts.

In sum, Albert Einstein's quote encapsulates his understanding of how attention, productivity, and distraction are interconnected. By eliminating interruptions, people can enter a zone of focused attention that allows their capacity for original thought and productive action to flourish. Against a backdrop of incessant interference, Einstein's advice continues to inspire dedicated concentration as people look to produce their own personal works of art.

In a modern landscape chock-full of constant connectivity and information overload, the ability to reclaim our focus is a precious skill—one that allows us to carve out sanctuaries of concentration within a sea of distractions. Just as a sculptor chisels away excess stone to reveal a masterpiece, the art of eliminating distractions empowers us to chip away at the noise and clutter that hinder our productivity: unveiling the true potential of our efforts.

Imagine a serene garden where carefully tended plants flourish in a space free from weeds and chaos. Eliminating distractions is like tending to this garden of your mind, a process that cultivates an environment where your creativity and concentration can thrive and the seeds of your goals can sprout unimpeded.

In this chapter, we'll embark on a journey of clarity and focus— one that equips us with the tools to identify and eliminate elements that divert our attention from what truly matters. From the psychology of distractions to the strategies that empower us to create focused workspaces and routines, we'll dive into the art and science of reclaiming our attention.

Whether you're striving to soar to new heights in your career, seeking to enhance your learning capabilities, or simply yearning for a deeper sense of presence in your daily life, the ability to eliminate distractions is a powerful asset that paves the way for productivity and personal growth.

Prepare to explore the realm of mindful engagement and undivided attention. In navigating the complexities that come with eliminating distractions, you will discover the art of creating spaces and habits that foster concentration, amplify your effectiveness, and lead you toward a life of purposeful achievement.

Together, let's embark on this journey of empowerment—one whereby the act of eliminating distractions is the canvas on which you paint the vibrant strokes of your undivided focus.

Eliminating distractions is a critical aspect of maintaining focus, boosting productivity, and achieving your goals. In today's fast-paced and digitally connected world, abundant distractions can significantly hinder your ability to complete tasks in an efficient manner. Taking proactive steps to minimize or eradicate disruptions can help you stay on track and enhance your concentration as you make the most of your time.

Here are some benefits of eliminating distractions (and how to go about it!):

Benefits of Eliminating Distractions:

1. Enhanced Focus: With distractions proven to fragment your attention and stifle your ability to concentrate on important tasks, eliminating them allows you to channel your focus and energy toward the task at hand.

2. Increased Productivity: Reducing distractions will help you complete tasks more quickly and effectively, sparking higher levels of productivity and a greater sense of accomplishment.

3. Better Time Management: Distractions consume valuable time—meaning tasks taking longer than necessary—and their eradication thus helps you both manage your time more efficiently and allocate more of the same to meaningful activities.

4. Improved Quality of Work: Focusing in the absence of interruptions feeds your ability to produce higher-quality work, as you can better engage in deep thinking and critical analysis practices.

5. Reduced Stress: Constant interruptions and distractions can contribute to stress and feeling overwhelmed,

meaning their elimination fosters a calmer and more controlled work environment.

Strategies to Eliminate Distractions:

1. Designate a Workspace: Create a dedicated workspace that is free from distractions. Use this space exclusively for work or other tasks that require a large degree of focus.

2. Turn Off Notifications: Silence notifications on your devices including smartphones, tablets, and computers. Notifications can disrupt your workflow and pull your attention away from tasks.

3. Use Website Blockers: Enlist the help of browser extensions or apps that block access to distracting websites or social media platforms during work periods.

4. Manage Email: Set specific times to check and respond to emails, rather than constantly checking your inbox. This prevents email from becoming a constant interruption throughout your day.

5. Set Boundaries: Communicate your need for focused work time to others and set boundaries to minimize interruptions. Give coworkers, family, and friends a heads-up about when you're available and when you need to concentrate.

6. Employ Time Management Techniques: Dedicated strategies (e.g., the Pomodoro Technique) encourage you to work in focused intervals, reducing the temptation to give into distraction.

7. Clear Away Clutter: A clutter-free environment can reduce mental distractions. Keep your workspace organized and free from unnecessary items at all times.

8. Prioritize Tasks: When you have a clear plan detailing what needs to be done, it's less likely unrelated tasks will sidetrack your thoughts and derail your plans.

9. Practice Mindfulness and Meditation: Engage in dedicated techniques to enhance your ability to stay present and focused.

10. Utilize "Do Not Disturb" Mode: Activate "Do Not Disturb" mode on your devices to silence incoming calls, messages, and notifications during designated work times.

11. Wear Headphones: Wearing headphones—even in the absence of music—can signal to others that you're engaged in focused work and thus discourage interruptions.

12. Set Specific Break Times: Plan and schedule regular breaks to address any potential restlessness and minimize the urge to fall victim to distractions.

Eliminating distractions is an ongoing effort that requires a large degree of self-awareness, discipline, and consistent practice. By implementing these strategies and customizing them for your own specific needs, you can create a beneficial environment that supports your focus, productivity, and overall well-being.

Step 7

PRACTICE SELF-COMPASSION

"Embrace the gentle strength of self-compassion, for it is the cornerstone of inner resilience and true personal growth."

-Nelson Mandela

Nobel Peace Prize winner and international hero Nelson Mandela is revered for his lifelong commitment to fairness and human dignity, one in which his fight against apartheid and call for peace and forgiveness went on to change the world forever. The quote above reveals his deep awareness of the human spirit and the role compassion plays in promoting both personal and societal development.

Born on July 18, 1918 in South Africa, Mandela spent his entire life fighting for equality and freedom from the repressive apartheid regime. During his 27-year imprisonment due to actions he took as a leader and activist, he never wavered in his commitment to justice and the worth of every individual. Following his release from prison, Mandela went on to become South Africa's first black president and worked tirelessly to promote unity and healing as the country moved away from apartheid.

Mandela's quote emphasizes the importance of self-compassion, a trait he embodied throughout his life. By showing yourself the very same compassion you'd show a friend enduring a rough patch in his/her life, you're practicing self-compassion. What Mandela means by "gentle strength" is accepting one's flaws and difficulties without condemnation and then addressing them with compassion and understanding.

The expression "cornerstone of inner resilience" highlights the importance of self-compassion in developing psychological fortitude. Mandela's personal experiences no doubt shaped his view on the significance of overcoming hardship, and self-compassion is a tool used to build the resilience and strength of character so essential for overcoming adversity.

The fact that Mandela recognizes a link between self-compassion and "true personal growth" demonstrates his faith in the power of this technique. Just as he advocated for personal development by promoting self-compassion, so did he champion societal development by pointing to the importance of reconciliation and understanding. Fostering genuine growth, greater self-awareness, and a more meaningful sense of purpose begins with cultivating a loving and forgiving connection with oneself.

Mandela's message of self-compassion aligns with his broader message of forgiveness and reconciliation, with the transformational power of compassion demonstrated by his capacity to show this not just to himself but also those who had persecuted him. Mandela ultimately became a symbol of resilience in the face of adversity and an inspiration to millions due to his capacity for self-compassion.

Mandela's words serve as a reminder to practice this kindness in today's hectic and demanding society, encouraging people to be as patient and kind to themselves as they would to anyone else and thus strengthening their character, fostering their self-development, and helping to create a more empathetic and equitable world.

In sum, Nelson Mandela's quote reflects the great wisdom and compassion that characterized his life: stressing the importance of self-compassion as the bedrock of emotional fortitude and genuine development and asking all to practice the same. In this way, his life and work testify to the transformational potential of empathy.

Within the tapestry of our lives, compassion often flows abundantly toward others though we may neglect to extend the same gentle kindness to ourselves. The art of practicing self-compassion, therefore, invites us to turn our reservoir of empathy inward: giving ourselves the same understanding, patience, and warmth that we readily offer those we care about. This is an art that fosters emotional resilience, nurtures self-worth, and provides a sanctuary of solace amidst all of life's challenges.

Imagine a gentle rain nurturing blossoms in a garden—petals unfurling, leaves stretching toward the sun. Practicing self-compassion is much like this nourishing rain, allowing our inner selves to flourish and thrive despite life's tumultuous storms. It's a reminder that just as we care for the world around us, we too deserve attention and tenderness.

In this chapter, we'll embark on a journey of self-discovery and emotional well-being—one that equips us with the tools necessary to cultivate a deep and abiding relationship with ourselves. From understanding the science behind self-compassion to embracing practical techniques that bolster our emotional resilience, we'll dive into the art and practice of self-compassion.

Whether you're seeking to shore up your mental health, navigate challenges and complexities in your relationships, or foster a more nurturing inner dialogue, the ability to practice self-compassion is a foundational pillar that supports holistic well-being.

Prepare to delve into the realm of self-love and acceptance. As we explore the intricacies of practicing self-compassion, you will uncover the power of nurturing your inner world, cultivating emotional equilibrium, and forging a profound connection with yourself.

Together, let's embark on this journey of empowerment—one wherein the act of practicing self-compassion weaves together a tapestry of emotional strength, self-discovery, and a deep appreciation for the extraordinary person you are.

Practicing self-compassion is a fundamental aspect of maintaining emotional well-being, cultivating a positive self-image, and nurturing your overall mental health. It involves treating yourself with the same kindness, understanding, and acceptance you'd offer a friend in times of difficulty or self-judgment. Ultimately, self-compassion helps you better navigate challenges, build resilience, and foster a healthier relationship with yourself.

Here's why practicing self-compassion is important (and how to integrate it into your life!):

Importance of Practicing Self-Compassion:

1. Enhanced Mental Health: Self-compassion reduces the self-criticism and negative self-talk often associated with anxiety, depression, and other mental health challenges.

2. Improved Resilience: When you approach yourself with compassion, you're better equipped to handle setbacks and failures and can develop a more balanced perspective/bounce back more readily.

3. Reduced Stress: Self-compassion helps mitigate the effects of stress by fostering a kind and supportive internal dialogue, leading to greater emotional equilibrium and lower levels of anxiety.

4. Boosted Self-Esteem: Treating yourself kindly and with self-compassion contributes to a positive self-image and higher self-esteem.

5. Motivation and Growth: Self-compassion encourages a growth mindset, as you're more willing to take risks and learn from experiences without the fear of harsh self-judgment.

Strategies to Practice Self-Compassion:

1. Mindful Awareness: Pay attention to your thoughts and emotions in the absence of judgment. Mindfulness allows you to observe your inner experiences without getting caught up in self-criticism.

2. Self-Talk Makeover: Replace negative self-talk with kind and encouraging language. Treat yourself as you would a friend, offering understanding and supportive words.

3. Self-Kindness: Be gentle and nurturing toward yourself. In the face of any challenges, extend the same kindness you would to a loved one.

4. Common Humanity: Recognize that *everyone* faces difficulties and struggles. Remind yourself that you're not alone in experiencing setbacks or imperfections in your life.

5. Self-Forgiveness: Acknowledge and forgive yourself for past mistakes or shortcomings. Remember that to err is human.

6. Self-Compassion Break: During challenging moments, take a few deep breaths and acknowledge your feelings. Remind yourself that suffering is a universal human experience and offer words of comfort.

7. Self-Care: Engage in activities that nourish your body, mind, and spirit. Prioritize self-care practices that promote your well-being.

8. Realistic Expectations: Avoid setting unrealistic standards for yourself. Embrace your limitations and acknowledge that you're doing your best, no matter what.

9. Gratitude: Focus on the positive aspects of yourself and your life. Express gratitude for your strengths and the progress you've made over time.

10. Social Support: Reach out to friends, family, and/or professionals if you're struggling. Accepting help is a form of self-compassion, after all.

11. Imperfection Acceptance: Embrace the idea that perfection is simply not attainable. Allow yourself to make mistakes and then learn from them.

12. Growth Reflections: Regularly ruminate on your personal growth and accomplishments. Celebrate your achievements, no matter how small they seem.

Practicing self-compassion is a journey that requires patience and self-awareness. By integrating these techniques into your daily life, you can foster a kinder and more compassionate relationship with yourself: leading to greater emotional well-being and a more positive outlook on life.

Step 8

REWARD YOURSELF

"Grant yourself the sweet indulgence of rewards; for in celebrating your accomplishments, you fuel the fire of ambition."

-Richard Branson

Richard Branson—British business magnate, investor, and philanthropist known for his risk-taking and creative strategies—launched the Virgin Group, an enterprise empire that now includes record labels, airlines, internet service providers, and even a space tourism company. The sentiment shared in this quote reflects Branson's view on the significance of acknowledging accomplishments and using them as inspiration for further development and aspiration.

Branson was born in London in 1950 and went on to found Virgin Records in the 1970s. This effort paved the way for the expansive Virgin name to be used in several fields, with Branson known as a pioneer in the economic world thanks to his fearless personality, willingness to take chances, and capacity to question established norms.

According to Branson, rewarding oneself can help foster drive and ambition. The expression "sweet indulgence of rewards" implies that recognizing and rewarding effort and success is more than just a nice bonus; people are more likely to keep working towards their goals if they feel encouraged by the positive emotions connected with their achievement.

"Fuel the fire of ambition," meanwhile, highlights the connection between acknowledging success and encouraging the drive for future accomplishment. Branson recognizes that taking the time to publicly recognize one's achievements serves as a powerful reminder of the rewards ripe for attainment via focused effort. The drive to continue growing and achieving is stoked by this constant reminder.

Branson's own entrepreneurial path reflects this focus on acknowledging success, with his capacity to both recognize and pursue new opportunities exemplified by the several sectors in which the Virgin Group has triumphed. From record-setting transatlantic flights on Virgin Atlantic to pioneering space tourism on Virgin Galactic, his businesses showcase his commitment to innovation and expansion.

Given this emphasis on always pushing forward, Branson's words serve as a reminder to pause and appreciate progress along the way while acknowledging that success is about so much more than just having fun; it's also about feeding our aspirations and propelling us onward. In rewarding our efforts, we can establish a positive feedback loop that keeps us moving forward.

Ultimately, Branson's quote sums up his thoughts regarding the importance of celebrating success in order to stay motivated. By delighting in the deliciousness of rewards, one can strengthen his/her commitment to develop—with Branson's outlook on business and life an example of how rewarding it is to both reflect on one's achievements and look forward to those in the future.

In the grand symphony of pursuit and accomplishment, the act of rewarding oneself acts as a harmonious interlude: a celebration of effort, moment of acknowledgment, and testament to the journey traveled. It is also a vital component of motivation, a practice that infuses our endeavors with a sense of joy, satisfaction, and the fuel necessary to propel us further along the path of achievement.

Imagine a traveler embarking on a long and arduous journey, each milestone marked by a resplendent vista or a moment of respite. Rewarding oneself is much like these markers of progress as a chance to pause, reflect, and imbue the journey with a sense of purposeful enjoyment. It's a reminder that pursuing our goals is not just about the destination but the meaningful experiences and personal growth that occur along the way as well.

In this chapter, we'll embark on a journey of affirmation and self-appreciation—one that equips us with the right tools to acknowledge our hard work and cultivate a positive cycle of motivation. From understanding the psychology of rewards to exploring creative ways to treat ourselves, we'll delve into the art and practice of self-reward.

Whether you're striving for professional success/personal growth or simply hoping to infuse your daily routine with moments of joy, the ability to reward yourself is a catalyst that can elevate your journey and amplify your accomplishments.

Prepare to immerse yourself in the realm of self-acknowledgment and gratification. As we explore the intricacies of rewarding oneself, you'll discover the power of celebrating even the smallest victories, permeating your pursuits with positivity, and weaving a tapestry of motivation that propels you toward continued success.

Together, let's embark on this journey of empowerment—one whereby the act of rewarding yourself becomes a melody of appreciation, inspiration, and a profound recognition of the remarkable person you are.

Rewarding yourself is a powerful and motivating way to reinforce positive behavior, celebrate achievements, and maintain a sense of accomplishment. Whether you're looking to achieve personal goals/professional milestones or simply check off tasks on your to-do list, incorporating rewards into your routine can boost your motivation, enhance your mood, and make the journey toward your objectives more enjoyable.

Here's why rewarding yourself is so important (and how to do so effectively!):

Importance of Rewarding Yourself:

1. Acts as Positive Reinforcement: Rewards serve as desirable stimuli for your efforts and accomplishments, creating a sense of pleasure and satisfaction and encouraging you to continue working toward your goals.

2. Boosts Motivation: Knowing a reward awaits can increase your enthusiasm to complete tasks or reach milestones as a tangible incentive that keeps you focused and engaged.

3. Celebrates Achievements: Rewards offer a means to toast your achievements, no matter how big or small, as an acknowledgment that enhances your self-esteem and confidence.

4. Creates Positive Associations: Linking tasks with rewards can make them feel more enjoyable and less daunting, thus reducing resistance and procrastination.

5. Encourages Progress: Establishing a reward system can help you track your progress and stay committed to a journey that feels more purposeful as you're working toward a prize.

Effective Ways to Reward Yourself:

1. Set Milestone Rewards: Define specific milestones or goals and attach incentives to each one. Celebrate reaching a certain level of progress or completion with a meaningful reward.

2. Treat Yourself: Plan enjoyable activities or treats you can indulge in after accomplishing a task. This could take shape as a favorite snack, leisure activity, or movie night.

3. Reap Physical Rewards: Consider buying yourself a small gift or item you've been pining for as a reward for completing a significant project or achieving a goal.

4. Enjoy Some Time Off: Allocate time to relax and engage in leisure activities you enjoy. This could be a day off, a spa day, or a weekend getaway.

5. Utilize Social Rewards: Spend quality time with friends or loved ones as a way to celebrate your achievements. Sharing your success with others enhances the joy that comes with your accomplishments.

6. Learn and Grow: Reward yourself by investing in your personal growth. Consider enrolling in a course or workshop that aligns with your interests or goals.

7. Seek Out Virtual Rewards: Use gamification apps or systems to earn virtual rewards, badges, or points for completing tasks or staying productive along the way.

8. Write a Positive Note: Leave yourself a heartfelt note of appreciation or encouragement. Reading these affirmations can boost your self-esteem and serve as additional motivation.

9. Utilize Creative Outlets: Engage in creative pursuits such as painting, writing, or crafting as a reward for your hard work.

10. Engage in Charitable Acts: Make a donation or contribute to a cause that is meaningful to you. Helping others is always a rewarding and fulfilling experience.

11. Reflect and Celebrate: Regularly take time to reflect on your accomplishments, big or small. Celebrate your progress and the effort you've put in.

12. Mix and Match: Combine different types of rewards to keep things interesting and maintain your motivation over time.

Remember to tailor your rewards to your preferences and what genuinely brings you joy. By integrating a system of incentives into your routine, you can create a positive feedback loop that fuels your motivation, boosts your productivity, and helps you achieve your goals with an increased sense of satisfaction and fulfillment.

Conclusion

As we wrap up this exploration into the realms of self-improvement, productivity, and emotional well-being, we find ourselves standing at the crossroads of possibility and potential. The insights we've uncovered, strategies we've embraced, and principles we'll ultimately weave into the fabric of our productive lives illuminate a path toward personal growth and fulfillment.

Throughout this journey, we've learned that setting clear goals serves as a compass to navigate the vast landscape of our aspirations. Breaking down daunting tasks into manageable steps empowers us to conquer challenges with confidence, while eliminating distractions allows us to harness the power of focused effort. By embracing time management techniques, we've uncovered the key to unlocking the full potential of productivity.

In practicing self-compassion, meanwhile, we nurture the seed of kindness within to foster a foundation of emotional resilience. We also recognize the act of rewarding ourselves as a powerful tool to celebrate milestones, motivating us to continue striving for excellence. With each thread of wisdom, we've woven a tapestry that depicts a purpose-driven, balanced, and successful life.

As we move on and away from these pages, we'll carry with us the torch of knowledge, fire of determination, and lantern of self-awareness: striding forward equipped with the right tools to shape our destinies, transcend our limitations, and embrace the infinite possibilities this wonderful life has to offer.

Hence, our journey does not end here; it extends into the very fabric of our actions, our choices, and our dreams. Let's continue to navigate the seas of self-discovery, drawing upon the insights we've gained to ride the waves of change with grace and resilience.

May the lessons shared herein be the wind beneath your wings, carrying you toward a future imbued with purpose, meaning, and unwavering determination as you embrace the canvas of life with open hearts, eager minds, and an unwavering belief that we possess the capacity to shape our destinies and create a legacy of growth, achievement, and enduring fulfillment.

Epilogue

As we bid adieu to this transformative journey through the realms of personal growth, productivity, and emotional well-being, we find ourselves at a vantage point—a place where reflection and realization intersect. The pages we have traversed contain a medley of insights, revelations, and actionable wisdom with the collective power to shape our lives in meaningful ways.

Just as a skilled navigator uses stars to guide a ship through uncharted waters, *we* have plotted a course through the unexplored territories of our aspirations with intention and purpose: setting sail on the seas of self-discovery in pursuit of our goals and learning to navigate the ebb and flow of time with finesse.

In chasing after our ambitions, we have harnessed the force of self-compassion as a beacon of light illuminating our path: nurturing our resilience and reminding us of the boundless benevolence residing within. The tapestry of self-compassion we've woven is one of healing, growth, and a deeper understanding of our intrinsic worth.

Through the art of eliminating distractions and fostering focus, we have sculpted a space where creativity and productivity flourish while embracing the power that comes with breaking clear goals down into achievable steps and celebrating every milestone as a testament to our dedication and determination.

As we stand at this crossroads, let us carry with us the lessons of these pages, the insights we've gained, and the practices we've embraced. They will serve as a constant reminder of our capacity for growth, ability to overcome challenges, and potential to create a life that resonates with purpose and fulfillment.

May the journey we've embarked upon continue to unfold, not just within the confines of these words but in every facet of our existence. Let us approach each day with intention, each goal with determination, and each moment with a heart full of self-compassion and gratitude.

The voyage does not end here; it continues as we move forward, armed with the tools and insights we've acquired. With a sense of accomplishment and an eagerness for what lies ahead, let us travel confidently into the unexplored territories of our future—one shaped by the transformative power of personal growth, productivity, and emotional well-being.

Endnote

As we draw the curtains on this exploration into the depths of personal growth, productivity, and emotional well-being, I am reminded of the power that resides within each of us. The journey we have undertaken—one of self-discovery, introspection, and empowerment—has illuminated the potential for positive change and growth currently lying dormant within our hearts and minds.

While these pages certainly offer insights, strategies, and techniques, the true magic lies in your willingness to embrace them, mold them to fit your unique circumstances, and take action. The journey of personal development is ongoing as a continuous cycle of learning, adapting, and striving for improvement.

As you move forward, remember that you are the author of your own story, the architect of your own dreams, and the captain of your own ship. The tools and wisdom you've acquired are your compass and map, guiding you through the uncharted waters of life.

Embrace challenges as opportunities for growth, setbacks as stepping stones to success, and each day as a canvas beckoning you to paint the masterpiece of your life. Continue setting goals, breaking them down into achievable steps, and nurturing a spirit of self-compassion that fuels your resilience and well-being.

May the lessons shared within these pages serve as a source of inspiration, guidance, and motivation as you navigate the complexities of existence. Continue to flourish, evolve, and impact the world around you in meaningful and positive ways.

About the Author

Matthew is a design architect and property developer by day and an ardent self-help writer by night. With a robust background in architecture and property development, Matthew brings a unique perspective to his work: combining creativity, business acumen, and a desire to inspire and empower others through his writing. He is also a dedicated proptech enthusiast and enjoys constantly exploring innovative technologies to enhance the real estate industry.

Matthew's varied life experiences have helped shape his fascinating and motivational persona. After studying architecture in Auckland, New Zealand, he spent more than 10 years working as a design architect in Singapore before shifting gears as a property developer in Thailand for the last 15 years. He is currently working to develop an online platform designed to simplify the real estate ecosystem.

Matthew's expertise extends beyond the realms of blueprints, building sites, and technology. Not only has he consulted numerous businesses—offering 1-on-1 coaching services and advice on general business, real estate, and technology—but he has also supported countless experts and amateurs alike as they seek to better understand their respective industries.

Matthew's path is proof of the positive impact that optimism, creativity, and self-assurance can have on one's life. His life's tale is a motivating example of how anyone can achieve his/her goals with the appropriate attitude and the drive to keep plugging away at them. Matthew's story has inspired people of various backgrounds to believe in themselves and their abilities and take risks in pursuit of their goals.

Current Book List:

- 50 Habits of Highly Successful Business Leaders (2023)
  The Roadmap to Success and Fulfillment

- Mastering the Art Of Business Networking (2023)
  The 8 Essential Steps to Creating Lasting Connections.

- Master Procrastination & Achieve Your Goals (2023)
  8 Essential Steps to Regain Control of Your Life

Matthew resides in Chiang Mai, Thailand with his wife and two children. You can reach out to him at www.linkedin.com/in/matthew-lin-72061b282. He would love to hear from you!